PAUL S. SCHUDER

Science Collections

Woodland Public Library

SAY NO AND KNOW WHY

"SAY NO AND KNOW WHY"

Kids Learn About Drugs

Wendy Wax

Photographs by Toby McAfee

WALKER AND COMPANY ✺ NEW YORK

First published in the United States of America in 1992 by Walker
Publishing Company, Inc.

Published simultaneously in Canada by Thomas Allen & Son
Canada, Limited, Markham, Ontario

Library of Congress Cataloging-in-Publication Data
Wax, Wendy.
Say no and know why: kids learn about drugs / Wendy Wax:
photographs by Toby McAfee.
p.   cm.
Summary: Follows students as they experience an antidrug program
involving activities such as watching nurses and doctors in action
and attending a drug trial.
ISBN 0-8027-8140-3 (cloth). —ISBN 0-8027-8141-1 (lib. bdg.)
1. Drug abuse—Prevention—Study and teaching—New York
(N.Y.) 2. Drug abuse—Prevention—Study and teaching—New
York (N.Y.)—Pictorial works. 3. Drug abuse—New York (N.Y.)—
Juvenile literature.   4. Drug abuse—New York (N.Y.)—Pic-
torial works. 5. Narcotics, Control of—New York (N.Y.)—
Juvenile literature. 6. Narcotics, Control of—New York (N.Y.)—
Pictorial works. [1. Drug abuse. 2. Narcotics, Control of.] I.
McAfee, Toby, ill. II. Title.
HV5809.5.W39   1992
362.29'09747' 1—dc20   92-150
                                        CIP
                                        AC

Book design by Georg Brewer
Illustrations by Brandon Kruse
Printed in the United States of America

10 9 8 7 6 5 4 3 2 1

ACKNOWLEDGMENTS

The author and photographer of this book would like to thank Dr. Nesta Quarry, Dr. Kem Louie, Dr. Ngozi Nkongo, and Dr. Rosanne Wille from the Lehman College Division of Nursing, and Bronx County District Attorney Robert T. Johnson for being so helpful. We'd also like to thank Court Officer Joseph La Grippa from the Bronx Criminal Court, and Nydia Negron, Vera Joseph, and the staff at North Central Bronx Hospital for all their understanding and cooperation. And a special thanks to Bronx County Assistant District Attorney Gary Klein for his "whatever you need" attitude and special assistance in creating this book.

This book could not have been created without the enthusiasm of the Bronx P. S. 16 sixth-grade classroom whom you see in the photos, and the support of their teacher, Angela Morgan, and principal, John Morales. To the class: good luck in junior high!

A DAY AT
SCHOOL

Sarah Johnson

A DAY AT SCHOOL

My name is Sarah Johnson, and ever since I was five years old, I've wanted to be a nurse. This morning I was excited to go to school because a nurse was coming to talk to our class.

It took Mrs. Morgan, our sixth-grade teacher, a lot longer than usual to quiet us down. Everyone knew that today we were going to start a special program about drugs. A man and a woman were sitting at the back of the classroom watching us. When we finally calmed down, the woman got up and came to the front of the classroom.

Hello, everyone. My name is Nesta Quarry, and I am an assistant professor at Lehman College, here in the Bronx. I teach people to become nurses. I'm sure you've all met a nurse at one time or another, haven't you?

We all said yes.

Do you all know what a nurse's job is?

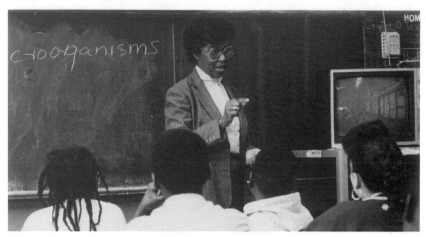

I had my hand up before anyone else. Dr. Quarry called on me and asked me my name. I told everyone about Chris, the nurse at my doctor's office. Chris gives me shots and blood tests whenever I go in for a checkup. Chris always has a new joke to tell me so I laugh instead of cry.

Mark, the boy who sits in front of me, said that nurses help doctors when they prescribe medicine.

Nurses do all that and more. They help give medicine, they comfort people, and they're always teaching patients how to get well and stay well. When a doctor prescribes medicine, the nurse teaches the patient about the medicine—how to take it and how often to take it. Where else do nurses work?

They work in schools, and hospitals.

That's right, but hospitals are big places. Where in the hospital?

We all shouted out answers—the emergency room,

the operating room, intensive care, the mother and baby units, blood donation centers.

I told everyone about the time I sprained my arm doing a flip in gymnastics and a nurse in the hospital's outpatient ward took care of me.

There are also nurses who work outside the hospital. Community health nurses work in stores, factories, insurance companies, and other businesses. Nurses also work in the army, navy, and air force, caring for people in the armed services and their families. Have any of you ever thought about becoming a nurse?

I raised my hand even before she finished her sentence. Some of the other girls in the class raised their hands too, but none of the boys did. That figures. Dr. Quarry noticed this too.

I don't see any boys raising their hands. Did you know that men can be nurses too? In fact, we need more men to go into the field of nursing.

A few boys made faces. They can be so obnoxious. I raised my hand and asked Dr. Quarry what you have to do to become a nurse.

First of all, you have to work very hard in school— especially in science and math. Nurses must be good in these subjects because they have to understand how the body normally works and what happens to it when people become sick. Nurses also have to understand how to prepare and give the correct doses of drugs to people to help them get well. You should also be good in English, because nurses must be able to communicate—aloud and in writing—with doctors and patients. It's great if you know more than one language.

I thought about the A I got on my last English test. I've also been doing pretty well in science. I promised myself that, from now on, I'd work extra hard in math. Then someone asked if you have to go to college to become a nurse.

You don't have to, but most people now attend college to become nurses. You do have to finish high school, though. You can go to college for four years and get one kind of degree, or you can go to a community college program for two years to get another kind of degree. In both cases, you graduate with a major in nursing.

Then are you a nurse?

Not quite yet. First you must take a special test to

become licensed. You cannot work as a nurse until you pass the test. Then you become a registered nurse, or RN, which means you can be a nurse in the state you live in. Being licensed means you're qualified to take care of patients.

I asked Dr. Quarry how much nurses get paid. (I need to know because I plan to have six kids, a dog, and a parakeet, so I'll have to make enough money to support them.)

That depends, Sarah. Years ago, when more people went into nursing, the salaries were much lower than they are now. Today there are fewer people going into nursing, so they have to offer more money to make more people interested in becoming nurses.

Sometimes a nurse can make more than $30,000 a year at his or her first job.

That made everyone in the class think about becoming a nurse—even the boys.

Finally, Dr. Quarry brought up the topic of drugs, which was why she had come.

One thing nurses must know about is drugs. Do you know the difference between drugs the doctor prescribes and illegal drugs?

We all answered at once: "When the doctor gives you drugs, they help you get well." "Illegal drugs might have some bad stuff in them." "You can get addicted to drugs you get on the street."

What's it like to be addicted to drugs? Does anyone know?

When you're addicted, you always want more of the drug. You feel like you're sick when you can't get it.

That's right. Now do any of you know how diseases are transmitted from one person to another?

I said that when someone with a cold coughs or sneezes on you, you can sometimes catch their cold. Or if you drink through the same straw as them.

Yes, but there are other ways that more serious diseases get transmitted or passed from one person to another. Some are transmitted from person to person by microorganisms (tiny living things) through the blood. If the blood of one person has these microorganisms and this blood gets into the blood of another person, that person will get infected. This is how many people who used drugs got the disease known as AIDS.

Everyone in the class had heard about AIDS.

When one drug user shares a needle with another who is infected with the AIDS virus, that person will most likely get AIDS too. What do you think happens when women who have AIDS have babies?

Don't the babies get AIDS too?

Yes, they do. This is because the mother may pass the microorganisms to the baby during the baby's birth. And since a mother's blood is shared with her unborn baby, the drugs get into the baby's blood too. Many times a baby is born addicted to drugs because its mother used drugs while she was pregnant.

Why would a woman who's pregnant use drugs when she knows she's hurting her baby?

When you're addicted to drugs, you usually care more about getting drugs than you do about your baby.

Are there any ways that nurses can stop the mother from taking drugs?

There are nurses who educate mothers and help them get information about prenatal care. Prenatal means "before birth"; prenatal care is for the mother and baby before the baby is born. This is the best way to make sure a woman has a healthy baby.

We were all more than a little surprised when Angela, a girl in our class who hardly ever says a word, raised her hand and asked if anyone helps the mothers besides the nurses.

There are lots of people who work in medicine, counseling, and education for the sole purpose of keeping mothers and other people off drugs or helping them to get off drugs. And all of you can end up working in one of these fields. Next week you'll be going to the hospital, where you'll see babies who are addicted to drugs. Are there any questions you'd like to ask me before I introduce you to Mr. Klein?

No one raised a hand. I was trying to imagine what the hospital would be like. It would sure be different than our usual field trips to the museum or the zoo.

Mark Stewart

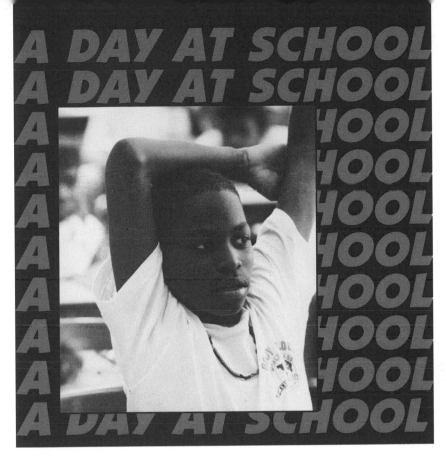

A DAY AT SCHOOL
A DAY AT SCHOOL
A
A
A
A
A
A
A
A
A DAY AT SCHOOL

My name is Mark Stewart, and in my opinion, the best thing about the first day of the drug program was listening to Mr. Klein, the lawyer. At first, I thought it would be boring, but it wasn't. Mr. Klein was really cool.

My name is Gary Klein. I heard most of your names when you told them to Dr. Quarry, but you may have to help me out a little. I'm an assistant district attorney, or assistant D.A., in the Bronx. Do any of you know what I do?

Jack answered that he thought Mr. Klein was like those guys on TV shows with policemen, lawyers, and arrested guys. (Jack watches more TV than anyone else I know.) Then he added that he

thought the policemen brought people that have just been arrested to Mr. Klein.

Yes. They're brought to me or to one of the other assistant district attorneys. What we do is prosecute the case. There are two types of criminal attorneys. Does anyone know what they are?

I knew the answer. I said that one attorney is on the

arrested guy's side and the other is against him.

That's right. The person who's been arrested gets represented by a defense attorney. That's not what I do. I do the opposite. A district attorney is a prosecuting attorney. My job is to make sure the entire truth comes out at a trial. I try to make sure that, if the person who's been arrested is guilty, the judge or the jury convicts him and sends him to jail. Another way of looking at it is that I send people to jail.

Wow. I wondered if he was ever afraid the criminals would come after him.

Does anybody have any idea how many assistant D.A.s there are, just in the Bronx?

Someone guessed two.

Close. There are 365 assistant D.A.s and one district attorney. Our D.A. here in the Bronx is Robert T. Johnson, and you'll all meet him in the last session of this program. I work with 65 other people in what is known as the Narcotics Division. We prosecute people who are involved with drugs.
    Let's say you want to become an assistant D.A. Do you know where you go after you finish the sixth grade?

That was easy. A bunch of us yelled out, "You go to junior high."

Then where?

High school!

Then where?

College!

Then where?

Law school.

Right. For how many years?

Jack said seven years.

Mr. Klein tried not to laugh to make him feel bad for answering wrong. But I could tell he found it a little funny.

Seven years would seem like forever. You only go to law school for three years. So after you've gone through high school, college, and law school, are you an attorney?

A few of us shouted out yes. I wish I hadn't been one of them, because Mr. Klein told us that you weren't an attorney yet. First you had to take a test called the bar exam.

The bar exam is a test you have to take that lasts two or three days. Once you pass the bar exam, you become an attorney.

That seems like such a long time to be in school.

It might seem like a long time, but it's really not. Do you know how long you can spend in jail for selling drugs?

I took a guess and said 20 years.

If you sell one vial of crack, you could go to jail for 25 years. How old will you be 25 years from now?

Most of us said either 37 or 38. Carol said 39, since she's been held back a grade. Everyone turned to look at her, and she turned bright red. I think she wished she hadn't said it.

Okay. If you get caught with four ounces of crack, how long can you get sent to jail for?

Life?

Right. You can go to jail for the rest of your life. So if a friend says to you, "I'll pay you $250 if you hold this cocaine or heroin for me. I promise you won't get in any trouble," what do you do?

I said that *I* sure could use $250 for a new bike. Everyone laughed—including Mr. Klein. Without me and Jack in the class, I think everyone would get pretty bored.

Yeah, but if you get caught with the drugs—just this one time—you can go to jail for your whole life. It doesn't matter if you're 16, 17, or 18 years old. You could be 40, and it wouldn't make a difference. You could end up spending the rest of your life in jail.

Does anyone know how long you have to do crack before you're addicted?

We all knew it didn't take too long.

There's no magic number, but for most people the first

time they use crack they are addicted. Let's say a friend says to you, "Come on over to the basketball courts Friday after school. A bunch of us are getting together," and you go. As soon as you get there, somebody whips out a pipe. The next thing you see is one of those little vials. Has everyone seen a vial at one time or another?

We all said yes. Sometimes we see empty vials in the street around our school—and it's not like we live in such a bad neighborhood or anything.

So you know there are green tops, blue tops, red tops, and gold tops. Someone says, "Take a hit of this—just one hit—and either you'll like it or you won't." Taking that one hit might take you to the end of your life—fast! I'm not trying to scare you. I'm just telling you the truth. The stuff goes right into your brain, and your brain says it wants more. Now you might say you don't want more, but your brain says you do. Taking this drug one time can easily lead to taking drugs many more times.

I knew I'd never do drugs, but I wondered if anyone in the class ever would. We all know there's drug dealing going on in our neighborhood. What if a drug dealer forced a kid to do drugs once, and then the kid became addicted? Man, that'd be tough.

Do you think you can make a lot of money selling drugs?

Everyone shouted yes.

You sure can. You can make $500, you can make $1,000, and you can make a whole lot more than that. Sounds great, right? But think about this. Do you know what the average age of death is for people involved in selling or using drugs?

Twenty-five?

You're right. Twenty-five years old. That's 12 years from now for most of you. How many of you want to live a little longer than 12 more years?

There was no question about it. We all raised our hands.

Say you make thousands of dollars selling drugs. What are you going to do with all that money when you're dead?

That was a weird question that made us think. For a few minutes the room was quiet.

What is it about drugs that makes people die so young?

We answered that you might get AIDS, or overdose. Then I said that you could die in a shoot-out.

All of you are right. Let me explain what Mark means by a shoot-out for those of you who don't know. Say

one person is selling red tops on your corner. Somebody else comes along and also wants to sell red tops on your corner. Now there's competition. How do they decide who gets to sell red tops on your corner? They use machine guns and pistols to shoot each other.

We were all quiet.

Now don't you think it's a lot easier and smarter to go through junior high school, high school, college, and law school than to turn around tomorrow and start selling drugs on your corner?

We all agreed. It seemed strange that less than an hour ago seven years of school had seemed like a long time. Mr. Klein really knows how to make a point.

Who has seen drugs being sold?

Some of us raised our hands.

What kind of drugs?

One kid said there was this guy who lived next door to him. One day the police came around to the corner, went up the stairs, banged down the guy's door, and took him away. He was selling crack.

What other drugs are being sold?

Different kids said heroin, marijuana, ice.

Are all those drugs addicting?

We all said yes.

Can those drugs kill you?

We all said yes—louder this time.

Then Mr. Klein asked us if we had any more questions. Jack asked how much money he makes. I had been thinking of asking that, but my mom told me never to ask that question. She said it's rude. But Mr. Klein didn't seem to mind.

When I first started working at the Bronx District Attorney's Office, I made $21,000 a year. Now, four years later, I make $41,000 a year. The district *attorney himself makes over $100,000 a year. Some attorneys make up to $400,000 a year.*

We couldn't believe it. If drug dealers knew that, maybe they would have decided to work harder in school to become lawyers!

Now I ask you, isn't it worth working hard in school and doing your homework every night?

We all knew the answer.

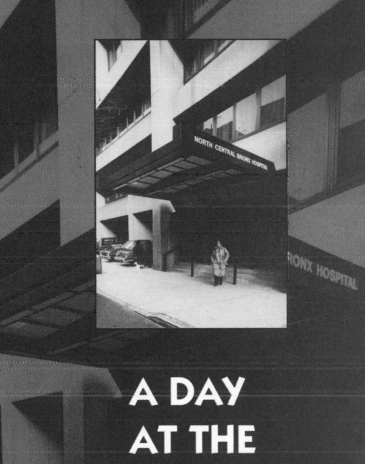

A DAY
AT THE
HOSPITAL

Mike Martin

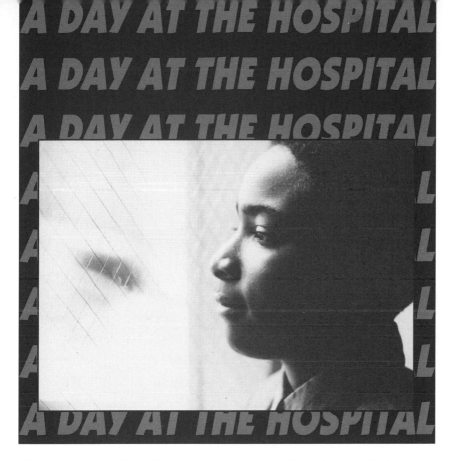

As we rode the bus to the hospital, I was thinking about what Dr. Quarry had told us about male nurses. At first, I had a hard time picturing it. But after learning about what nurses do, I think it might be cool to be a nurse. I'd never say this to any of the guys—at least not now. But maybe one day more men will be nurses, and it'll seem more normal. Maybe one day I just won't care what the guys say. Nurse Mike Martin—not bad.

Doctors and nurses were everywhere in the hospital. Most of them smiled at us as we passed, but some were in too much of a hurry. Dr. Quarry was waiting for us on the seventh floor.

Before we start today, I'd like to hear what some of you think we're going to see today.

27 ▶

Some kids said sick people, and others said people with AIDS. I said we'd probably see people who got AIDS from taking drugs.

The hospital is filled with people who have gotten AIDS from taking drugs. But today you're going to see mostly babies. You'll have to be very quiet so you don't disturb them.

Dr. Quarry split us into four groups, so there wouldn't be too many of us in one place at one time. Brian, Richard, Lisa, and Sarah were in my group.

It was hard to keep quiet as we walked through the halls. Nurses and doctors rushed around with stretchers, pushing them through groups of people talking. We saw a boy with a nosebleed and a

mother holding a little girl who wouldn't stop crying. Finally we got to our first stop—the Mothers' Unit.

When a woman finds out she's pregnant, she comes to the hospital. A nurse tests her to see if she's been using drugs so we know if we have to worry about the baby's health. Babies whose mothers use drugs get sick easier than babies, and they cry a lot more. Babies whose mothers are crack addicts tend to be so tiny they can barely stay alive. If the mother has been using drugs, we pay special attention to the baby's health when it's here.

Can a mother who uses drugs have a healthy baby?

Yes, she can, but if that's the case, we worry about the baby's life at home after it leaves the hospital. Why do you think this is so?

If a mother uses drugs, she'll spend money on the drugs instead of on things the baby needs.

That's right. What else?

None of us knew, but the answer was simple.

If the mother is all messed up on drugs, she won't be able to take care of her baby. When the baby cries, she won't know if it is hungry or hurt or needs to have its diaper changed.

I was about to ask why they don't just keep the babies in the hospital until the mothers get off drugs, but I thought she might think it was a dumb question. But then Brian asked, and it didn't seem so dumb after all.

We'd like to keep the babies here, and some hospitals do. It's just that there are so many mothers on drugs that we don't have room to keep all of their babies until they get off drugs—if they get off drugs. Some mothers leave the hospital without their babies and don't come back. We keep the babies here until we can find someone to take care of them. We call them boarder babies. It can take a long time to place a baby, so sometimes we have them here for almost a year.

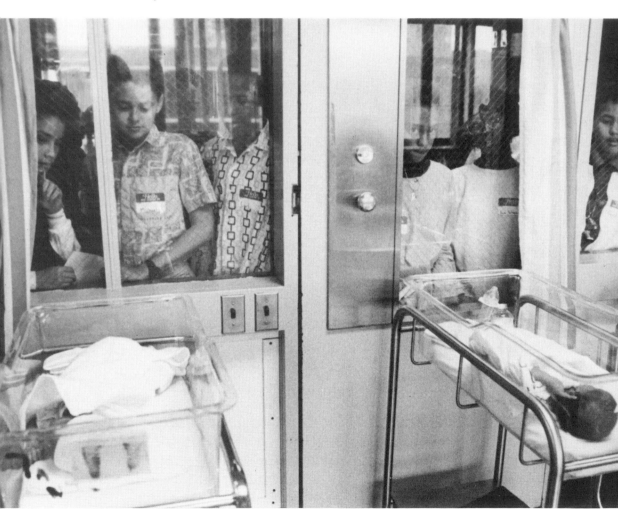

She led us over to a big glass window. Behind the window was a room full of tiny babies wrapped in white blankets and lying in plastic beds.

These are the healthy babies.

Then everyone was talking: "They're sooo cute." "Look how tiny that baby boy's feet are!"

Quiet down. You don't want to disturb them. Their mothers came to the hospital as soon as they knew they were pregnant. They were examined by a nurse practitioner to see if they and the baby inside them were healthy. The nurse practitioner tells mothers how to take care of themselves up to the time the baby is born. She tells them what to eat, how much sleep to get, and how much exercise to do. She also tries to get them to quit smoking, drinking alcohol, and taking drugs.

The babies sure were cute. I don't remember my little brother being this cute when he was born. I just remember him crying a lot and smelling bad. Most of the babies were sleeping. Every once in a while, a baby would wake up and cry. Then a nurse wearing a yellow gown would come over and check to see if that baby needed to be changed or fed.

One of the other groups came to the window we were looking through, and Dr. Quarry led us over to the sick babies.

The mothers of these babies took drugs, and now the babies can get sick very easily. That's why they have to be in isolation units or incubators.

One kid said that he couldn't look and another one

said that it was really sad. The rest of us were quiet. We just stared at the most awful sight in the world. The sick babies were *nothing* like the healthy babies. For one thing, they were much smaller. Most of them were in separate plastic containers that looked like square bubbles.

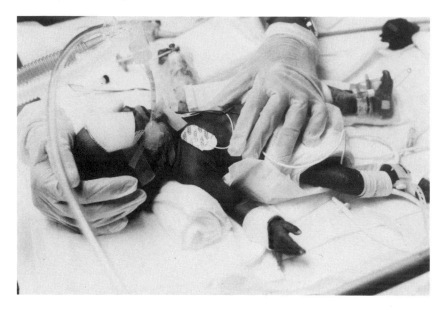

It was noisy in there, probably because most of them were crying. I pointed to one and said it looked like he was real hot. It was so sad. I felt like I was going to cry, so I looked away from the window at the wall. I said, "Don't cry, don't cry," to myself, over and over and over again. It worked a little. But when I looked up, I noticed tears in Sarah's, Lisa's, and even Brian's eyes. I looked back at the babies and let myself feel sad.

The hardest part of a nurse's job is having to watch the babies struggle. The most rewarding part of the job is when we are able to help. The babies depend on the nurses and doctors here to stay alive.

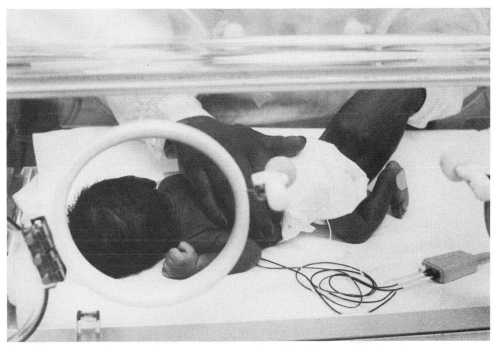

Dr. Quarry showed us a room that had one baby by himself. The baby was no bigger than my hand, and he was shivering. His chest was moving up and down, like he was working really hard to breathe.

Before I ask a question, I usually think it over and plan out exactly what I'm going to say. I don't want the other kids thinking my question is stupid. But before I realized what I was doing, I asked Dr. Quarry why there were tubes up the baby's nose and so many wires attached to him.

One tube helps him breathe, and one tube helps to feed him. The wires are taped to his chest so we can keep track of his heartbeat.

This baby's mother is a crack addict. When a mother is addicted to crack, the baby inside her becomes addicted to crack. When the baby is born, its body can't get the drug from the mother anymore, so it gets very sick. That is why it is shaking.

I asked her why the baby was so small.

It's small because its mother didn't take care of herself while she was pregnant, and this caused problems. This baby had to be born two months before it should have been. It never had a chance to develop all the way. It weighed less than two pounds when it was born. Doctors are happy when a baby is six or seven pounds.

Are babies ever born so small they don't live?

Only a few of the babies born this small survive. But even if they live, their brains and their bodies are probably damaged for the rest of their lives.

Again someone asked how a mother could take drugs knowing that it could do this to her baby.

No one said anything. Dr. Quarry led us back to the front of the hospital, where we came in. Along the way, she showed us where kids our own age stay when they have to come to the hospital. We couldn't stop remembering those tiny, shivering babies and thinking about how hard their lives would be—just because their mothers had used drugs.

We met up with the other three groups in a room with lots of chairs. There was a long table with chocolate chip cookies and orange juice for us. We were all hungry and ate a lot, but I'll bet the cookies would have tasted better if we hadn't seen the sick babies first.

When everyone was seated, Dr. Quarry introduced us to a social worker and two doctors. They told us all about their jobs and what working in a hospital was like.

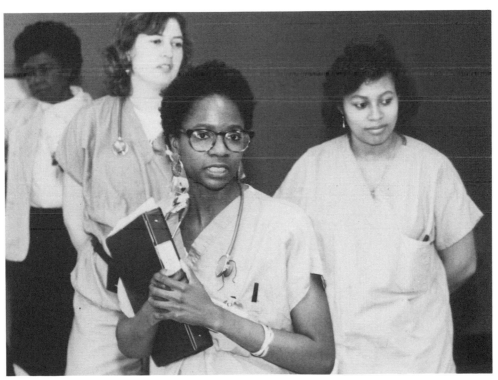

Finally it was time to go. While we waited outside the hospital for the bus, I counted up seven windows from the sidewalk. That's where the sick babies were. I looked around me and saw Brian and Sarah and some of the others were looking up there too. I wondered whether any of the babies would make it to sixth grade. And if they did, what would they be like?

A DAY
AT COURT

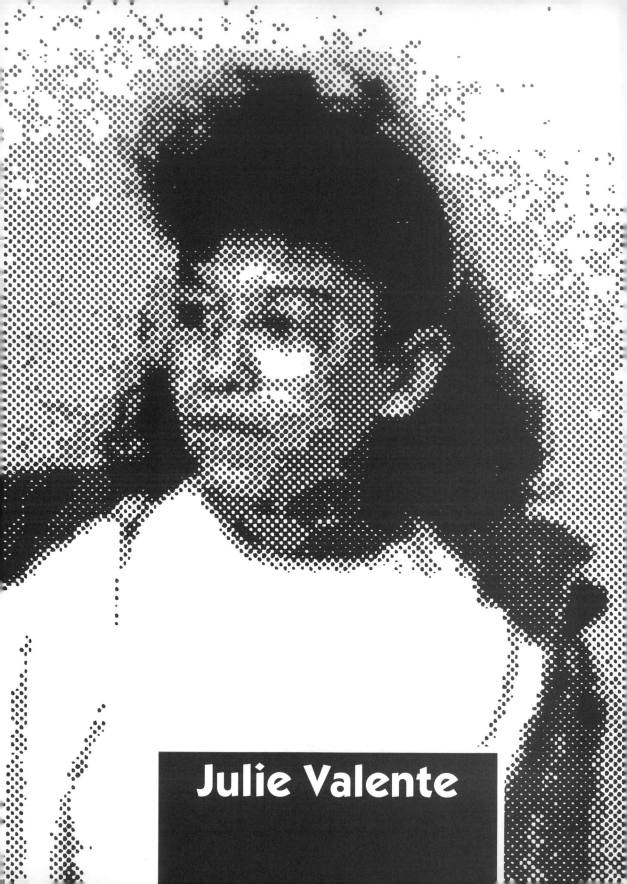

Julie Valente

My name is Julie Valente, and to me, coming to the courthouse seemed much more exciting than going to the hospital. My mom's a nurse, so I hear all about what goes on in the hospital and with drugs and stuff.

When we got off the bus, Mr. Klein said we were at the criminal court. Everywhere we looked we saw men and women wearing white shirts. Almost every one of them was carrying a gun and a radio. A man came up to us and introduced himself as Officer La Grippa.

Most of the people you see dressed in white shirts are court officers. That's what I am. Today's going to be a busy day for you. Follow me, and I'll show you around a little.

39 ▶

Officer La Grippa took us around to the other side of the building, where we saw a kid wearing handcuffs. He didn't look like he was much older than us. A policeman was guiding him through the door. I knew it wasn't right to stare, but I couldn't help it. He was swearing and didn't look too happy. Someone asked where the policeman was taking him.

He's taking him to central booking, which is behind this door. That's where police take suspects who have just been arrested.

I asked what they were going to do to him.

First they'll take his fingerprints. Then they'll take a picture of him—a mug shot. While this is happening, the policeman who made the arrest will go downstairs to a room called the complaint room and tell an assistant D.A. what happened.

Then what?

Then the assistant D.A. decides what crime to charge the person with.

What happens to the guy who was arrested—the suspect?

Well, after the mug shots are taken, the police put the suspects in pens, where they stay until they go before the judge. See that door? It leads to the pens. There's another door that leads from the pens into the courtroom.

It would have been cool to see the pens! I asked Officer La Grippa if he'd take us there, but he said no.

The pens are much too dangerous for you to see. It's a small, dirty place where people have no privacy. There's only one toilet. If you have to go to the bathroom, you have to do it in front of everyone else. The people argue and fight a lot. If there's a bench, only the biggest and strongest people can sit on it. The others get stuck sitting on the floor.

We all looked at one another. No way were we ever coming here! Officer La Grippa led us back to the front of the building. There were metal detectors just like the ones at the airport. But we didn't get to go through them since we were with Officer La Grippa.

We're going into a courtroom now, so you'll have to be very quiet. I'll explain what's going on, but you'll have to sit close to me since I have to whisper.

The first thing I noticed in the courtroom was that the judge was a woman.

Everyone who's arrested in the Bronx comes through a courtroom like this one. The judge sees people who have just been arrested and decides if they should have to post bail.

Bail is money that a person has to put up to make sure he comes back for his trial. If the person arrested is able to post bail, he can go free until the day of his trial. If he shows up for his trial, he gets his money back. If he doesn't show up, he loses the money and the police go out to find him and arrest him again.

Mark was pointing at a door near the front of the courtroom. A guy was bringing someone in.

They're coming through the door that leads to the pens.

The man walked over to the table in front of the judge. He didn't sit down. It was kind of hard to hear what was going on, but I got some of it. Officer La Grippa leaned down and explained to us what was happening.

First the assistant D.A. told the judge he thought bail should be $5,000. Then the arrested person's lawyer told the judge why he thought the person shouldn't have to post any bail. The judge agreed with the arrested person's lawyer, so the arrested person can leave until his trial.

The man must have been happy that he didn't have to go back to the pens. We watched him walk out through the same doors we had come in.

Next, four people came before the judge. Two of them were in handcuffs. They talked to the judge for a few minutes and then went back through the door they came from.

Why can't *they* leave?

Because the judge just told them they must post bail. Since they don't have it now, they have to wait in jail until a family member or friend brings in the money. The judge has the right to set whatever amount of bail she feels is appropriate for the circumstances. She can also set no bail at all, like she did a few minutes ago.

I asked what happens to a person who can't pay the bail—like if it's $5,000 and he just doesn't have it.

He has to stay in jail until his case comes up.

Someone asked if the judge gets to keep the bail money.

No. When a person posts bail, that money is held by the city. When the case is finally over, the bail money is returned to the person who paid it.

If the guy doesn't show up when his case comes up, the judge issues an order for his arrest. This is called a bench warrant. The police go looking for him, and he doesn't get the bail money back.

Officer La Grippa signaled to the judge to let her know we were leaving. The judge stopped everything so we wouldn't disturb anyone.

When we got out into the hallway, Mr. Klein explained how the whole criminal court system works. He showed us a chart like this:

Criminal Court System

1

PERSON ARRESTED.

2

ARRESTED PERSON TAKEN TO POLICE STATION.

3

FINGERPRINTS TAKEN.

4

PERSON TAKEN TO CRIMINAL COURT BUILDING.

5

WRITTEN COMPLAINT PREPARED BY AN ASSISTANT D.A. SAYING WHAT CHARGES ARE.

6

A LAWYER ASSIGNED TO REPRESENT THE DEFENDANT.

7

DEFENDANT BROUGHT BEFORE A JUDGE.

8

AN ASSISTANT D.A. MAKES AN APPLICATION TO HAVE BAIL FIXED. BAIL IS NEVER PAID RIGHT AWAY. THE DEFENDANT'S LAWYER ARGUES FOR NO BAIL OR A LOW BAIL.

9

THE JUDGE EITHER DOES OR DOESN'T SET BAIL.

9A

IF THE JUDGE DECIDES NO BAIL IS REQUIRED, THE DEFENDANT CAN LEAVE UNTIL HIS TRIAL.

9B

IF THE JUDGE DECIDES BAIL IS REQUIRED, THEN THERE ARE TWO OTHER POSSIBILITIES.

9B1

IF THE DEFENDANT CAN'T MAKE BAIL, HE HAS TO BE IN JAIL UNTIL HIS TRIAL.

9B2

IF THE DEFENDANT CAN PAY THE BAIL, HE GETS TO LEAVE UNTIL HIS TRIAL.

10

IF THE CHARGE IS A MISDEMEANOR (SHOPLIFTING, SIMPLE ASSAULT, DRUG POSSESSION), IT IS TRIED AND DISPOSED OF IN CRIMINAL COURT. MORE SERIOUS CHARGES GO TO A GRAND JURY IN THE SUPREME COURT.

Mr. Klein took us over to the Supreme Court Building. We took elevators upstairs, walked down a hallway, and went into a courtroom. This time, the judge at the front was a man.

That's Judge Hecht. The people standing in front of the judge are the defendant and his lawyer. Can any of you tell me what is going on?

It's kind of hard to hear what they're saying, but I think the judge is telling the man what his rights are.

That's right.

I asked Mr. Klein what the guy was arrested for. He said that the guy had been carrying a pistol.

I heard the man agree to plead guilty. Then the judge told him that by pleading guilty he was giving up his right to a trial. The judge asked the man how old he was, if he had a job, and whether he lived with his family. Then the judge sentenced him to probation.

Do any of you know what probation is?

I do. It means he doesn't have to go to jail, but he can't break the law anymore or he'll be in real trouble.
  The man walked out of the courtroom staring straight ahead of him, like he couldn't wait to get through the door.

Mr. Klein took us into a small room behind where the judge sits. We waited for Judge Hecht to come in and talk to us.

Judge Hecht introduced himself and asked if we had any questions about what we'd seen in the courtroom.

Why would anyone plead guilty when he could have a trial where he has a chance of being proven innocent?

The man you saw in the courtroom did what we call plea bargaining. He pleaded guilty because he thought he would be found guilty if he had a trial. The sentence he'd get if he had a trial would be much worse than what he gets if he pleads guilty now and doesn't have a trial.

Then someone asked Mr. Klein what his job is.

I try to dispose of as many cases as I can, like I did

with this man, by plea bargaining. Plea bargaining is when the defense attorney and the assistant district attorney stand before me. The assistant D.A. tells me the facts of the case and recommends what punishment the person should receive if he pleads guilty. For example, if the defendant pleads guilty, the assistant D.A. might recommend that he go to jail for five years. The defense attorney recommends that the man, his client, not go to jail at all. He tries to get his client on probation—maybe he's only 16 or 17 and has no prior record.

Then it's my job to work out something that I feel will be best for both sides but that both attorneys will agree to. If the two attorneys can agree on what the person's sentence will be, the person pleads guilty— just like the man you saw in the courtroom. If we can't work it out by way of a plea bargain, the case is sent to a trial.

I still couldn't understand why the assistant D.A. would want to plea-bargain. If he put the guy on trial, he could probably convict him and he could put the criminal in jail for a much longer time. So I asked Judge Hecht about it.

We use plea bargaining because there are so many cases in the Bronx—about 11,000 or 12,000 a year— and there are only about 35 judges sitting on the supreme court. Since trials take a long time and are expensive, we plea-bargain to limit the number of cases that go to trial. It saves a lot of time and a lot of money. It may not be the best way to deal with the cases, but it's necessary.

Then we listened to Judge Hecht tell us how he came to be a judge. I asked more questions than anyone else, beginning with how he started out.

I started out, many years ago, going to public school in the Bronx, just like you. Then I went through high school, college, and law school and took the bar exam. I began working in a law firm. Then I became an assistant D.A., just like Mr. Klein. Five years later I was elected to the New York State Assembly. Then I was a civil court judge for 12 years. Last year, I was elected to the supreme court, and now I'm a supreme court justice. Any of you can do what I did—there's no reason why you can't. But you have to study very hard.

What if you don't want to become a judge—say you just want to stay a lawyer?

Not everybody becomes a judge. Actually, there are very few of us. But there are thousands of lawyers who enjoy practicing law, enjoy working for different firms, and enjoy their profession. When I started practicing law, I didn't plan on becoming a judge.

Someone asked the judge how much money he makes. So many kids in the class *only* care about money. But I guess I care about it a lot too. I want to make a lot of it so I can do anything I want to do.

I make $95,000 a year.

Maybe I'd try to become a judge. I could see doing it if I get tired of being a lawyer—just for a change. It would be fun to wear the long robes and say, "Order in the court!"

Are there any other questions?

What's the worst part of your job?

Unfortunately, I'd have to say that I get a lot of 16-, 17-, and 18-year-old kids before me who are here for serious crimes. Most of them have dropped out of school, and some can't read or write, so they can't find a decent job. The only way they can get money is to go out into the streets and commit a crime.

It's extremely important for all of you to stay in school and receive an education. That's the most important thing to remember from your day here in court.

A DAY
IN TRIAL

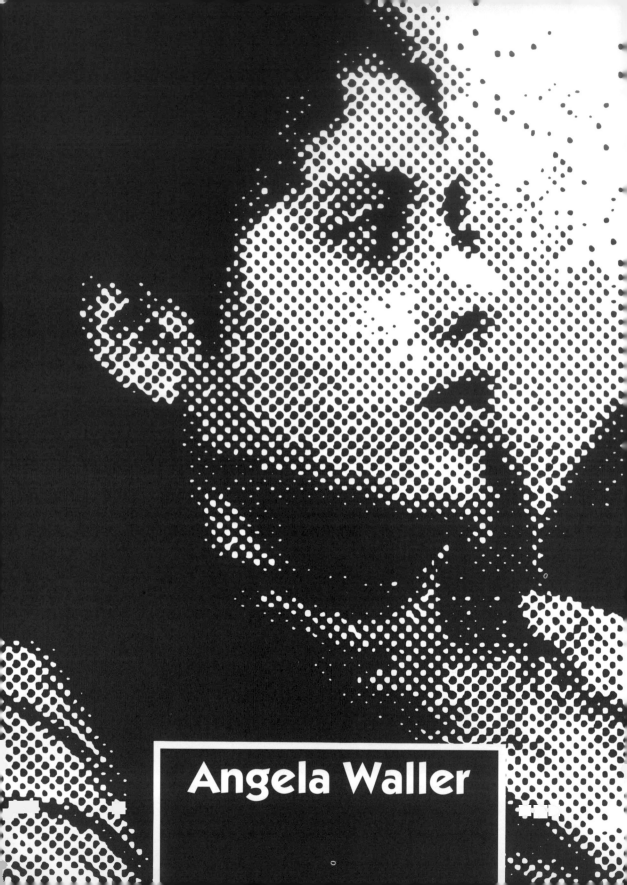

Angela Waller

A DAY IN TRIAL
A DAY IN TRIAL
A DAY IN TRIAL

On the last day of the drug program, we took the bus back to the criminal court. It was time for the mock trial. A mock trial is just like a real trial, but it's not real. Instead of there being a real judge, lawyers, and other court people, the kids in the class pretended to be these people—as if we were putting on a play. We spent four days rehearsing. At first, just thinking about it made me nervous. Shy Angela is what most of the kids call me, even though my real name is Angela Waller.

Mr. Klein gave each of us a part. While he was calling out our names, I was secretly hoping that by the time he got to "Waller" there wouldn't be any parts left. Then I could sit and watch. But that didn't happen. I was assigned to be a member of the jury. That, at least, wasn't as scary as being made a

lawyer and having to stand up in front of everybody. But then Mr. Klein told us someone on the jury had to be the foreman, the person who would inform the court officer when we reached a verdict, or decision. Steve Corker, another jury member, recommended *me*, and before I could say no, it was too late. I was the foreman or, in my case, the forewoman.

There was a certain trial procedure we had to follow. First, the court clerk had to swear in the jury. We each took the oath he gave us.

My heart was beating real fast when the judge asked if I would uphold and follow the law. I answered "I do" like everyone else did. Then the judge spoke to the jury.

It's up to the prosecuting attorney to prove beyond a reasonable doubt that the defendant actually committed the crime he is charged with. The burden of proof is on the prosecuting attorney.

A few weeks ago, I wouldn't have had any idea what he was talking about, but now I knew that he was saying the defendant is innocent until proven guilty.

Next, the prosecuting attorney and then the defense attorney read their opening statements. In the statements, each attorney told us what he or she intended to prove. The prosecuting attorney told us she was going to prove that a teenager named Norman Bates was guilty of selling crack. The defense attorney told us he was going to prove that Norman Bates was innocent. Then the prosecuting attorney called her first witness— Johnny Brown—to the stand. This was the beginning of what's known as the people's case.

Johnny Brown, like everyone else who spoke before the court, had to be sworn in. Then he was asked to point to Norman Bates, who sat at a table facing the judge. Next, the prosecuting attorney asked Johnny Brown questions about what took place on the day of the arrest. This is called direct examination. Here's some of what Johnny said:

On May 19, 1989, at 3:35 P.M., I was hanging out in front of my school. I saw this guy walking up and down yelling, "Red caps." Then I saw a Spanish girl walk up to the guy and give him money in exchange for something the guy took out of a paper bag. Then I saw another guy walk up to the same guy, and the same thing happened. I went into the school and told the school guard that I thought the guy was selling drugs. The guard called the police. When Police Officer Garcia came, I pointed the guy out to him. Officer Garcia went up to the guy, but he saw us and ran, dropping a brown paper bag. Officer Garcia picked up the bag, looked inside, and saw many vials of crack. Then he ran and caught the guy.

After hearing what Johnny Brown had to say, I felt that there was no question about it—Norman Bates was guilty. But one thing we'd been told again and again was that everyone is innocent until proven guilty. The defense attorney started cross-examining Johnny Brown. When he asked him questions like "You didn't actually *see* anyone exchanging drugs— just money. Is that right?" it seemed like Norman Bates could be innocent. When the defense attorney couldn't think of any more questions to ask, he said, "No further questions, Your Honor."

Then, one by one, three other witnesses were called up to the stand to be questioned. First came the school guard, then Police Officer Garcia, and then the chemist. The school guard and the police officer were asked to point to Norman Bates. The chemist was there to prove that he'd tested the vials in the brown paper bag and found them to be crack.

The only physical evidence the prosecuting attorney had was the paper bag with the crack vials inside. Before they could accept it into evidence, the police officer had to identify the bag and show how it was connected to the case.

After the prosecuting attorney had called all the witnesses who said Norman Bates was guilty, it was time for the defense's case. The defense attorney was trying to show that his client, Norman Bates, was not guilty. He started his case by calling Norman Bates as his first witness. Even though it was only Brian, I was starting to believe that this person had actually been selling drugs. The defendant was sworn in.

First he was questioned by his own attorney, then by the assistant D.A., the prosecuting attorney. Here are some things he said:

I was standing in front of the school talking with
some friends. Then I saw this kid over on the
playground selling crack out of a paper bag to
older kids. I saw him sell at least two times, and
I saw the kid take the money. I went right up to
him and told him he shouldn't be doing that,
and I tried to take the bag from him. The kid
started cussing at me and wouldn't give up the
bag. Finally, I grabbed the bag, and he ran into
the school. I'm holding the bag, and I see it is
filled with crack vials. As I was leaving to call
the police, a police car pulled up, and there was
the kid pointing his finger at me. Next thing I
knew, I was under arrest—I hadn't done
anything.

I couldn't *believe* how different this story was from
the other one. Could he be lying? Especially after
swearing to tell the truth, the whole truth, and
nothing but the truth, so help him God? It was

unbelievable. One of them was lying. Steve looked at me and rolled his eyes. I think it was because it was obvious that Norman Bates was lying—but I couldn't be sure. I guess everyone on the jury has their own opinion.

After Norman Bates was questioned, the defense attorney gave a summation, or closing argument, to the jury, telling us that his client, Norman Bates, was not guilty. Then the prosecuting attorney got up and told us that Norman Bates *was* guilty.

Finally it was time for the jury to make a decision. We went into a corner of the room and started talking about everything we had seen. All but two of us voted the same way. Then we had to convince them that we were right. We argued back and forth, and finally we got them to change their minds.

We had reached a verdict. I got up and stood

before the judge. I took a deep breath and made my announcement. I felt very important telling the court that we, the jury, found the defendant, Norman Bates, guilty of selling crack.

I knew this was only a mock trial, but I felt great. Mr. Johnson, the Bronx district attorney, gave us all certificates for completing the program. I felt that the jury's decision was the right one and, if this were a real trial, a crack dealer would have gone to jail. Having one less crack dealer on the street could save the lives of adults, kids, and especially innocent babies.

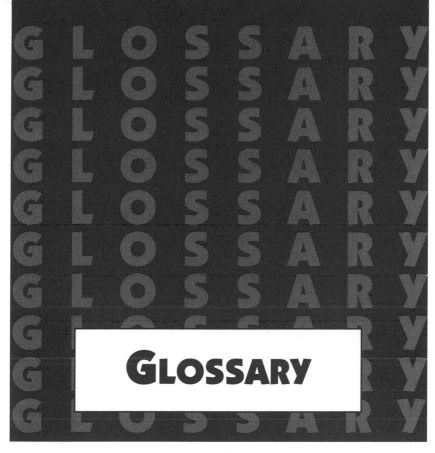

GLOSSARY

Addiction: A craving for certain drugs, which makes it hard for people to stop using them.

AIDS virus: A disease that attacks the immune system until the body can no longer fight off infections.

Bail: Money that a person arrested for a criminal offense is required to give to the court to obtain release from jail until his or her trial.

Cross-examination: The questioning of a witness by the opposing side to test the truth of his or her testimony.

Defendant: The person accused in a criminal case, or the person against whom recovery is sought in a civil case.

Defense attorney: A lawyer specializing in representing criminal defendants.

Isolation units/incubators: Special sterile environments where sick and premature babies get oxygen, food, and blood until they can survive on their own.

Jury: A fixed number of people authorized by the court to listen to evidence and decide questions of disputed fact.

Laws: Acts of a legislative body that must be obeyed or observed.

Microorganisms: Living things that are too small to be seen by the naked eye.

Plea bargaining: The process by which the prosecuting attorney and defense attorney in a criminal case negotiate the charge, against the defendant, subject to the court's approval.

Probation: The suspension of a prison sentence of a person convicted of a minor criminal offense, on condition of good behavior, under the supervision of a probation officer.

Prosecution: The proceeding by a prosecutor with a criminal action against a defendant until the conclusion of that action.

Prosecuting attorney: The public official who is appointed or elected in a particular area to conduct criminal prosecutions on behalf of the state.

Trial: A hearing conducted by a judge, sometimes with a jury, to determine issues between parties in civil or criminal suits.

Verdict: The formal decision or finding of a judge or jury on submitted issues of fact.

Witness: A person who testifies about his or her knowledge of something in a court of law. One who personally sees or perceives an event and is called to testify about what he or she saw or heard.